State of Reflection

Poetry

Jennifer Imani Luiru

State of Reflection

Poetry

Legal deposit - 1st quarter 2021
Library and Archives Canada / Government of Canada
Bibliothèque et Archives nationales du Québec, 2021.

© Editions AFRIKANA, 2021
Montreal, Quebec
CANADA

Image by Graphist and Operator Printing machines solvent/eco-solvent de
Pixabay
wallpaperaccess.com

ISBN 978-2-924928-15-8

DEDICATION

To my beloved Auntie Gracia who prematurely left us, but whose genuine kindness impacted all those around her.

ACKNOWLEDGMENT

I would like to thank my wonderful parents for their love, guidance and support.

To my brothers and sisters whom inspired many of my poems,

To my grandparents, cousins, aunts, uncles and friends who have always been there for me,

To Mrs. Safiatou Dicko Ba for her continuous encouragement and mentoring,

Finally, to the whole publishing and editing team whom helped bring this book to life,

Thank you !

FROM THE AUTHOR

The Silent Voices, Poetry, Afrikana, 2019.

CONTENTS

1. CAN YOU DO IT?

A question that is demanded
Upon your mind
The ongoing test
Feel the pain
Or fall among the rest.

A path of energy
Slowly drained
Creating regret
The flames.

By the second
It spreads throughout
The mind and body
Filled with doubt.

Can you do it
A second more
Or stumble down deep
within the earth's core.

Painfully crying,
Will you withstand the push?
The thought of pleasure
To take the break
But just moments away.

Breathe in the fire
Holding you back
To reach higher
Far from your grasp.

Become with all
The pain you saw
Embrace the last of your energy
Water's call.

For when you done
Washed with relief
Strengthened in belief
Can you do it
Yes, you can.

2. BLINDED

It is true that many can see
The beauty of the world
But may still happen to flee
Blinded in the world.

It was said being blinded isn't being blind
For there are many blinds ones who see
The weight that is put in one's life
The need to give out a hand.

The life with eyes put in sand
Or to view in the eyes of one's mother, father
But those who are blinded
Clearly don't see.

3. THE BOX

The norm of beliefs
The living in same
The path at your feet
The very one aimed.

The very thoughts lost
Founded in one's young age
Where the nonexistent box
Was never by the mind bought.

Where faith was free
To believe any believed
Yet here we stand
Blinded in the box.

And yes of course the box
A wonderful lad
Setting the standards
Logic as goals.

For those that step
Knocking upon the box walls
Breaking each reflected glass
Holding you back.

See the unseen
Seek the impossible

Living in their thoughts
Outside the box.

Venture the puzzled folks
Broaden the mind
Live in their imagination
Found beyond the meaning.

Those that do
Sit among the gods
Think ever so silently
Outside the box.

4. LISTEN

A simple order
It sometimes never done
Then again, it's screamed at you.

To hear the sound of nature
While one's mouth never stirs
To walk upon the woods
Stepping upon the leaves
Or the rain as it mourns
Pouring among the trees.

To hear the sound beyond the music
One picked based on the like of one's taste
The sound of your body moving along.

To hear the last heartbeat
The pound among the chest
To hear the last very whisper
The very last word said.

To hear the sound of silence
The very voice within
The simple cycle of inhaling and exhaling
The sound of heart
For there may be something you have never heard
So, Listen.

5. GREED

To like ones
Not owned by you
A possession of theirs
That you treasure too.

Some may be antagonistic
To whom they admire
Blinded by the unknown greed
With hatred and fire.

And there are those
Reverent to those above
Yet still sink below
Drowned in one's fame.

However, greed can be found in all
To look beyond and reach
For greed may not remain in all
There are those that hold
And fall no longer.

6. COMPARE

A fault among us beings
Sometimes needed to survive
To pick the best choice
One to keep you alive.

For to compare
You then make your choice
One you may regret.

To compare the options given
The door open
Made by your own will.

Or to compare the ones
You believe are below
Of one man
Whom call themselves as I
Which is simply needless
For the scale to compare
Is non-existent.

To compare one's skills
Or one's mind
To improve oneself.

Or to compare one's skill
Or one's mind

To live in greed of pride
Soon needed to be reclaimed.

To compare one's life for the better
Or the worst
It's a choice, you choose.

7. DARE FOR THE RISK

You' re sweating a lot
Thinking in thoughts
To take a chance
Uncertain of the forthcoming.

To drive among the path not taken
To break the norms
To live outside the box.

You call upon my name
Will you dare to risk ?
For the better Or for the worst
Will you take a chance?
And play my game.

Will you live in regret?
Or fame
For it is not I who rolls the die.

It is you who calls upon my name
Will you dare to risk?
For a destiny of enlightenment or dread
Play my game.

But of course, it's you who decides
The ultimate mind of all
To turn the twisted fate

You will be one to rise or fall.

So, will you
Take a chance
Roll the die
And play my game.

8. WE GIVE THANKS

It is for those who care
For those who given
Those that lifted spirits
Ones who brought smiles.

We give thanks to the very air
To the shrubs that grow
The very weed
One that eats upon the very tree.

For the seasons that pass
From chilly breeze
Summer's sol
Autumn's leaves
Spring's call.

To the wet and the dry
For the wind in the sky.

For those who loved
Those who raised
For those that showed you
The right path.

To the beings of all
For those of the past
For those of the present.

For those in the existing time
We give thanks.

9. THE SKY IS THE LIMIT

We have told
The young, the old
The sky is the limit.

And yes, very true
For those that knew
The sky is very high.

And this wise fellow
That calls himself the Sky
Lives above a friend of his
And vowed to never die.

I was told the Sky goes on
Into the infinite space
And yes, the one
Whom named the Sky
Mind beyond its span.

And it was once said
The sky had met a man
One that reached the Sky
With his very own will
He was to fly.

And although it's true
Sky never ending

Within the infinite Grace.

It was this human's mind
Never ending
For it reached the Sky
Beyond the Sky
Is one man's mind to fly.

10. A STRING

A string is long
So long
Among all its twists and tangles
A path is shown
Your fate
Yet to be woven
When walked by your feet
A choice you choose
A place you meet
And as the distance
Ahead comes
To an end
It's when you view
The lines and paths you took
Out and open
Choices chosen
The string then asks
What you think
Was life ever so short
Or was life complete
When living fullest.

11. LET'S PLAY

A game of cards let's play
Will you join son
Yes, you may
A game of fairness
A game of trick
To trust or flip
Which shall you choose?
As you meddle
Start your own path
Or hide in the meadows
A game of cards
A game of light
Lose it all
It won the fight.

12. COURAGE

Can't, just to grasp for hold
Own the very last
Under cries so very bold
Reach through the past
Aim for the final seconds sold
Give the very best
Earning a heart more than gold.

13. FEUD BETWEEN COLORS

Many of us wake up to the wonders of colors
Woven by the work of sight
While some may see two
There always seems to be light
And even those that don't see
Can view the brightness of the heart.

Colors are truly fascinating
Can describe
But not be described
It's limitless amount of types
Splendidly diverse.

A world of its own
Possessing the unknown feelings
As of red as rage
Green as good
Used to describe
Used to live.

An unlimited number it represents
Colors
Living in the views of mind
A simple blessing that awaken us in day
From the beginning to the end.

So, the young questions why

The color of skin
Is judged among us
For colors don't fight
They collaborate to create harmony
And we, being the paint of picture
Must own the very unique color seized
And paint the very place
For we are all different but same.

14. THE WILL OF WATERWAYS

With the will of water
And way of the will
An open path
Waiting to fill
Like a free spirit it runs
Not a moment still
Found in the plains
Lives in the hills
Benign to all
Its journey not to fall
As it runs
Free
Pure
Strong willed
Let the waterways open a path.

15. LAUGHTER

All giggles and grins
A smile to no end
Its humor's win
When one's face
a simple fix is all it needs
To let out the smile lying beneath the tears
Letting rooms fill with joy
An unknown agreement with one another
To let a laugh
And to live a full life.

16. PASSION IS MY POEM

To follow your own
Passion alone
The view of a plain along a sweet path.

To pursue the dream
Light like a beam
The sight of where you should walk.

It's the passion that flies
The passion that drives
In harmony with the soul's hymn.

Where fear is none
Fighting is fun
The potential of passion within.

Where passion is pain
Life a game
A path you choose to follow.

It's the passion that flies
The passion that drives
In harmony with the soul's hymn.

Yes, there will be struggles
Among a rocky path
To walk with determination itself.

And to walk upon barriers
To smile and never stop
To keep trying, ingredient of one who never fails.

It's the passion that flies
The passion that drives
In harmony with the soul's hymn.

Of course, you will fall
But a ladder you'll withdraw
To continue the path of passion.

Certainly, some will beat you down
Done to make you frown
Ratify and take your crown.

It's the passion that flies
The passion that drives
In harmony with the soul's hymn.

The power possessed in one passion
Each truly vast
To move in the path of one's own fashion.

Passion that ever lasts
For if one does not sit
He moves on his path a bit.

It's the passion that flies

The passion that drives
In harmony with the soul's hymn.

17. TO PROTECT

It is not to keep hidden
Rather, keep from
Not to leave the truth
To admonish instead.

Not to be watched by eyes
But fight the lies
Not to keep the palms clean
But to dirty them.

Not to go against adversary
To let them feel pain.

To protect
Is to strengthen
The mind and body above all
For if you do
A duo of both
Not one but two will be truly protected.

18. JEALOUSY

I like too much
That I don't own
I envy such lives
But antagonistic upon mine.

I look and see Desires
I think I need
But drowned in greed.

I don't look at me
And as the world is filled with many hope
As much as despair
Life will remain as never fair.

But blinded by wanting
There are others who'd wish
For someone to care
And even if we have everything
We would want a bit more.

However, we are humans
Where wealth defines person
Rather than character.

So, although made by envy

Instead reach a goal
Live your life fullest.

19. PERFECTION

Some say practice makes perfect
A lie we are told
Because there is no perfect
In the world we mold.

There are expectations of superior
However there's a sight one must seek
For there is always someone better
That contains something worse
Which allows none to be perfect
In the world we mold.

Some stay days
Others take decades
Mourning to be perfect
When the line will never exist
In the world we mold.

For even the best makes mistakes
So it's better we just learn
That it is a lie told
That one is perfect
In the world we mold.

20. WHY

Here you stand
A question you demand
Just why.

When your heart beats
Like soft waves
Left dumbfounded
Just why.

And those statues watch
Too bewildered to speak
You're left alone again
And as the truth is hidden
Just Why.

It's only you standing
You are withstanding the whip
It's every but you
Yet you still get hit
Just Why.

The only left desire
But bound to be abandoned
Hurting behind
Whom wished the truth to be spoken
But lions over a mouse
It is a guaranteed loss
Just why.

Can't the light change
Can't the darkness run
In an endless abyss
You descend in the deepest depths
Of your own very soul
Just why.

You ask
And as if you're left
On a cliff one finger hanging
You close your eyes to despair
And open them to hope
The view of infinite light
Washed in the warmest waves
Just why.

A question you demand
As you continue to walk
On the path ahead
Deep in buried ground
Just why.

21. CHANCE

Those who wish upon
The very one
Giving millions of doors
Wide open
And like a game of cards.

It you who chooses
To take a risk
Will you walk right in
Or let it descend
One chance is gone
Wasted or utilized.

When you can bear a fall
Or welcomed by gold
It you who carves their clay
Will you walk right in
Or let it descend
And two chances gone
Wasted or utilized.

Leave for a zero
Or try a 50/50
Guess your best
It's your choice after all
Will you walk right in
Or let it descend
That's three chances gone
Wasted or utilized.

And in a destiny of freewill
One that you direct
The fate lies in your hands
As chance is a friend
It's a foe as well
Where time and balance is key.

Once you walk in
A door of chance
One closed as well
For everyone is given
An equal amount of chances
An equal number of doors
Regardless where you start.

But as the path narrows
The millions of doors closing
It's you who chooses
To rise or fall
Or even to twist a handle
Or to knock upon a door
When you step in lives of chance
Where Time and balance is key.

22. PATIENCE

Only a matter of time
You have to wait
For own good sake
like a blooming flower
You rewarded with the power
When patient.

And as the clock's hands runs
Left in utter silence
Seems as if years pass
For when you look back
It's gone in a flash
When patient.

23. IN ABSENCE

When left without
Nothing sought
Yet in the presence of absence
You wish past was the route.

When left in absence
Of an item
You come upon its potential.

When left in absence
Of life one lived
You remember its presence.

In absence
Of love
You wish to be loved.

In absence
Of Happiness
You seek memories to smile.

In absence of life
You ask for more time
Yet it cannot be given
But searched
For purpose
To live the fullest.

24. COVID-19

While fighting in fear
Hiding for help
The unseen adversity
Dwells within anything
And with the simplest touch
You fall ail in its clutch.

Yet in this season that springs blooms
We protect the loved
Seeking things to do
Washing away boredom
And as rooms filled with laughter
We soon forget about the misfortune
That brought us together.

We discover new uses
Come up with plans
Learn to sanitize
And wash our hands
We look beyond our country
Yet remain cautious.

Day after day
We talk to worried scholars
And explain we are okay
But those that have fallen
Still remain in hope

For the Covid-19
Will not be the reason to mope.

And yet some courageous workers
Doctors and more
True heroes in the battle against Covid-19
Though we still keep praying
Under the golden candlelit
That it will fly away
The dreaded Covid-19.

25. WHEN MY TEARS HAVE DRIED MOLTEN

It hits hard as a rock
And crumbles as dry sand
When all I have worked for
But left to cry
In the darkest depths
Of my very own soul
When my tears have dried molten.

When I question humanity
Question reality
Of the very own paper you fold
All wrinkled up at the end of the line
Left as nothing known
But Me down deep
When my tears have dried molten.

In the battlefield
The crimson blood
The fear of the sight I see
The reflection of nothing but me
As shards pierce as I flee
Left as nothing known
When my tears have dried molten.

And maybe I prefer

To be that nothing
For nothing is me
No matter how far I seek
Will anyone understand
What I really feel
When my tears have dried molten.

As my heart erupts
The flow of it burning deep
With its carved scars
That I wish to never keep
Like a river they flow
Where no one knows
When my tears have dried molten.

26. THE STAIRCASE

You all started on a step
Some are very little stones
Whether it's the choice to move
Up or Down
My steps become your zone.

And on these exquisite steps of mine
A path that you must find
There is a floor
With a few doors
Which lead you above or below.

But fear not
Chances are infinite
Till your very last breath
What floor have you climbed
Shall you ever regret.

Will your young start
On a boulder than a stone
Or will you fall
To a pebble alone.

What is true about your steps
Is that you choose destiny
And I make reality
We work hand and hand.

Will you break barriers
On floors and continue to stand
Are you the one who will better land?
While every fate differs
It's you who paints gray skies.

Will you be known as the dot on a pebble?
Or the pebble that became a boulder
For every being there are infinite steps
It's just how far one can climb.

27. THE UNBREAKABLE WILL

It is an aspect found in children
But as we grow it's often lost
The words "never give up"
Their only thoughts.

When we view these willful eyes
Adamant to stand and walk
Caring less for their burning thighs
To let thoughts and sounds out to talk.

The enthusiasm for little
Things we take granted today
And strong will
That can carry you many ways.

28. PAINTING RED CRIMES GREEN

The intense animosity
Brought upon a being
The boiling hatred in one's heart
Yet to cover up these sins.

Then lie from the start
Just a bucket of paint
On a canvas stained deep blood red
And yet they paint over these crimes.

With a good coat of green
Then lie from the start
That you are not in fault
To cover the innocent
In a dark coat of blood crimson
Yet they were green from the start
Starting off with one lie.

29. THE BLAME

Blame
With nothing to gain
To remain in fame
A lie that is told
To be viewed as sane.

But a game with fires flame
Speechless dumbfounded
Quick to respond
Pointed fingers
No one is fond.

And yet you throw the lies
The tricks, the pranks
And weigh down
The thing now destined to break
Just to lie to oneself.

And soon the truth will come to light
Because a blame is a blame
A game with fires flame.

30. SUNRISE

It's clear
Blinding
The luminance of sunlight.

Sign of new
Fresh beginning
As the morning birds
Sing their melody
And welcome the sun.

The clouds white
Among the warm orange skies
Simply pure sight
Sign of new.

A bit different day from the past
As you move forward in the future
A path of life
And its gifts of day
Every sunrise.

31. BETRAYAL

The faithful trust
Plunged in dust
The second your back is turned.

You were there till the end
What caused them to send
You, to unthinkable outcomes.

The act of selfishness
To benefit oneself
Yet to hurt another
In a bond now rust.

When you break barriers together
It's faithful trust
Plunged in dust
Played right in a fellow friend's hands.

32. NEVER ENOUGH

We often wait too long
Thinking knotted strings
Will magically be a straight line.

And you rather enjoy simple pleasures
Then brace for the bumpy path
But as time runs before you
And fate makes abrupt movements
It's just never enough.

33. RIDING REGRETS

We find fault in others
Yet more in ourselves
To turn back time.

And take hurtful words
And actions made
We all have them
Regrets.

They leave us in a dark opaque abyss
We wish to escape
Your very own twisted path
From your very own past.

Yet with time destiny has given
Look forward and walk straight
Because there in no time to mourn the past.

34. ASSUMPTIONS

Can stab deeper than knives
Can burn hotter than lava
To think you know
To create a whole scenario.

When the real ones down below
Does it hurt to ask
To have a piece of my mind
But at the bottom
I can't speak
Over a head so high
I burst in tears of truth.

The voice that can't speak
Over a head so high
You have spoken for
But it's not these that break me
If all humans were saw as the same
Confident to speak
Honest to core
They wouldn't exist
To assume.

But humans are imbedded with thoughts
Each having their own shoes
You always plot something new
Whether in the near future

Or what you dream
No one can think your thoughts
Yet assume them
Can make a heart rot.

When all evidence turns against you
Yet you still will to speak
Over a head so high
No one will believe me
It's true we all assume
But it's better to ask
Then to start fumes.

To assume
Can stab deeper than knives
Can burn hotter than lava
To think you know the whole scenario.

35. QUESTION MARK

It's times like these
When you simply don't know
Our minds blank
Nowhere to go
Do you reside in the darkness or light?
Are you wrong, or right?

Yet what's truly the art of me
A question you see
Is that you find
A game I play with the mind.

But with the infinite possibilities
Of what you can ask
They can be answers as false or as fact
But as your curious mind wonders in my realm
Drowning in the many, many questions
Questioning the very quest of a question.

36. THE DREAMER BEARER

I will stand by you
Through thick and thin
Listen to you
And all your sins
Show you a start
A path you finish
I will watch you dream
Like I once before
And as we run in rocks together
I watch you soar
And as my line approaches an end
The will of a dream bearer
Is now in your hands.

37. TIME'S IS RUNNING OUT

Time can neither be bought or sold, yet it is given to
every being.
It's wished for often less or more, the moments filled
with "good and "bad"
Make each second matter, think before you act and
live with no regrets.
Ever year you grow older the more that the time
matters to you.
Seconds pass, then minutes, hours, days, weeks,
years, centuries, eternities

Running with no end, an hourglass with sand slowly
falling
Utilize time as if it's all you have left
Nor a friend or enemy it's just watching
Nonetheless it's them, that knows the end
Interested in how one thinks thoughts
Never is enough for you
Gasping for a breath

Out of words
Until then
Time

38. WHAT IF WE KNEW

People don't know
Billions of things
What if we knew
The purpose of our life
Shall we achieve it blindly?

Or if we knew
The end of our time
How would you use it?

If we knew
Everyone's secrets
Their thoughts
Why we search for love
What leads us to drop
What is there to fight for
Is it worth shedding blood for
Are we living right?
But we don't know
From the moment we were born
Unable to depict the differences of wrong and right.

We don't know
And we'll never know
Knowledge runs infinite
A race we could never finish
However, no one will stop you

To chase the impossible
To know
If we knew.

39. THE MAKING OF A DREAM

There are moments you have to treasure
Ones you wish you remembered
Telling you
A bridge can be built beyond the waves
Starting with a dream.

You must begin with a stone at a time
Before you can walk through the door you wish
to find
But the going is tough
Without the grit
The rock will be rough.

You settle for a simple life
Or aspire to reach higher
The spark the flame, the fire
When we believed endless possibilities
Needless to say
Before you miss the train
Hop earlier for a better time.

40. BENT TO THE BONES

What if for every lie
Yours bones bent
A small white lie
The tiniest dent.

It starts as a child
When the lie spun out
Nothing wild
No need to shout.

But as we grow older
The more we lie
The truth becomes colder
Soon out of sight.

Yet twisted lies
Meant to affect others
Have hurt you as well
Bent to the bones.

41. REGRET

A shadow of doubt
It creeps and crawls
Doubles itself
When night falls.

It follows you
Down the path
Stresses you
As giggles and laughs.

Sleep sweet dreams
Ruins your thoughts
The karma from
The fights you fought.

Try to think floods are mind
The wrong you've done
It's shows a sign.

You wonder why
Just why
Of all the paths
Why.

Ruled over regret
Runs without restrain
Utter most domination

To be your own disgrace.

While life runs its way
To be your own threat
Choose the right path
Run without regret.

42. PROCRASTINATION

I will
You won't,
Another form of no.
We, lowest of beings can lie to others
And to ourselves.

I will
You won't
You just say so
We the creatures with no form of leashes
A life lead on our own.

I will
You won't
To rush at the end
Without guidelines
You will wait after the term.

I will
You won't
We crave for comfort
Living without patience
Enjoying the now and destroying the next.

I will
You won't
Its ruins are success

Overcome the now
Conquer the next.

I will
Yes, you will.

43. BLOOD

A deep red crimson
Liquid yet thick
Cold as it flows
The wound you lick.

Within this battle
Let it be
Physical or within
We often shed the blood
The stream that runs in.

It lies between life and death
A moment wished not to see
As it punctures our skin
We forget how to breathe.

As it runs as a part of you
The color crimson red
As it pouts out and it covers you
Why shall it be shed.

There still lies a mystery
Of the blood Crimson red
Whether it flows with life or death
There is nothing to be said.

44. THOSE THAT DON'T HEAR

Often you pick sight over hearing
Because with sight you can see
Is it why you don't listen?
Yet there is many I offer you
Those that listen
As the sounds flow through your head.

We hear the rustle of the trees
Whistle of the wind
The melody of the music
Rhythm of rain
Screams of pain
The waves of water
And the sound of silence.

The little voice enclosed in our hearts
Can you hear it
Can you, your thoughts
Your true colors.

And can you hear beyond
Not measured in distance
But farther
For those that hear.

45. MASK

It's invisible
Yet we all have it
As it covers our face
A smile we think fake
Yet we wear it
For when it is broken
We see the beast.
That lies within.

For we're all a slave to something
And like makeup
It can be worn heavy
Or light
Because
We are all creatures
With different desires
And we feed upon them with greed
Our mask protects us
Until it breaks.

Look how we've become
Broken
This mask
Made of glass
Has many layers
It covers the real version of us
Break them

And you'll see the beast within us.

46. BLINDED IN TEMPTATION

All humans have desires
And tricked into falling
In an endless black hole of despair
Left with no stairs to climb.

It's the punishment
Of endless desires
Forms of pleasure
Greed
And lies
That you are dragged into
As a shortcut to comfort
Yet there are no shortcuts in life
In no life ever lived.

47. REMINDED IN A STATE OF A CALM MIND

Please don't remind me
It runs through my head
You fed my regret
I can never forget
The more you say
It shatters my mind.

Don't repeat my memories
Don't let it spread
It doesn't hurt
Till it echoes through my head.

Please don't remind me
I ought to be dead
Your words don't ache
Then I say it myself
A smile worn fake
An invisible rope
It strangles my throat.

Please don't remind me
I already know
You don't believe me
My mind ought to explode
I can't change my past

The one I die over
Dreadful memories last
A clear mind must takeover
Let the devils in my mind pass over.

Please don't remind me
Until I am fine
Then you can remind me
Of the fault of mine.

48. THE BETRAYAL

I trust you
As if I were old
I trusted you
Even though lies have been told.

I believe you
Blind you would still tell
I believed you
But down the cliff, I fell.

I have faith in you
That even if I said no
I had faith in you
But you pressed that blade on my throat.

I have hope
That you were different
I had hope
But your intentions were the same.

Your fake masked smile
Lead me here
Backstabbing me
It brought me to tears.

I trust you
With all my heart and soul

I trusted you
Yet I fell for a fool.

49. IN THE STATE OF REFLECTION

Maybe that's when it started
The peak of my life when you thought I was so
perfect
That I could never fall
But I bet you didn't know
That although I was a mountain
I was never Mount Everest.

Maybe that's when it started
I realized I wasn't any special
The talent couldn't compare
Yet you had, hope, hope, hope,
I had tried, I swear.

Maybe that's when I realized
I had no friends
And my intentions were never to be exposed
I was a beautiful vase filled with water
Patterns of bright gold
Decorated with roses
No one knew and no one will know
Through the white pure glass
Was water, filled with blood.

Maybe you never knew

Perhaps, I'm crazy
Every time I pushed through the doors
I thought of my goal
But to be reminded
I'm not at all special
I'm like every leaf in the fall
Just a mere brown leaf
That walked through the hall.

Maybe you thought I was emotionless
You are certainly right
But that just your view
From the outside
My thoughts are glorious
Ones that never lie
I'd seal my mouth
Rather than let them fly
They are ruthless, painful,
A stab to the heart
So perhaps I'm a clown
With a beautiful girl as a mask
But I switch between them
Like one without a name
Can't tell if it was false or a fact.

Maybe, when I realized
How rotten the world is
And I vowed to myself
To keep my siblings pure
Before entering the dark side
I was curious yet I gagged

Disgusted
But with time I came to accept
The huge difference between
Man and woman.

Maybe you never knew
I hated it
From the expectations
Why was it a boy was to work?
Yet a girl was to clean
We are not lowly beings
All I sought for equality
If I was angered washing the dishes
Why wasn't it him but me
For if all we were made for
Was to raised kids
There would be no point in my life
To become a maid of the house.

Maybe you never saw me
I walk with guilt and shame
Every wrong I do is a stab
I will never be the same
With time yells wouldn't show expressions
Whips wouldn't make me cry
And the assumptions
Things I most despise
Was like opening a wound with salt
To burn
Who said that?
To burn

Since when
To burn.

Maybe it's because you assume too much
That to ask it won't work
Without uncovering the truth
Pointed fingers were put
I am not perfect
Nor am I smart
You'd rather expect the worst
Then to be let down instead.

Maybe I am a ticking bomb
Soon to self-destruct
Everything that motivated me
Was lost
I was numb
Didn't desire anything
Confused
Lost
There was no joy
Walked on an empty path with no goal
And slowly slipped from the peak of the mountain
I was once on
So, I accepted it
Now lie in a state of reflection
Because my desire to live is fading
Care not if my life ends here
So, what is my drive
For every story to have an ending
Except for mine.

Maybe you never realized that
Every poem has a bit of these emotions
Emotions of anger, regret,
Soon I won't be able to embrace myself no longer
But you'll never understand
That runs through this glorious mind of mine.

50. COLOR ON OUR SKIN

Opposing forces
Its ultimate darkness and death
Vs the bright rays of light in our sight
Black and White
Colored in between
The very shades that describe humans of this world.

Our lives have started before us
From the name, status, wealth, family
It's a matter we could not discuss
But as a human who carves their path
These beginnings are superfluous.

But when did it start?
When did it go on?
For being a shade darker
Is something to shame upon.

Children of pure innocence
It doesn't make sense
Childhood should be merry
Never this tense.

Why should they worry
about something they can't change
When did they think?
"Mommy, is being darker strange?"

Black and White
A feud they fight
For a reason left unknown
A war for color
"All people are equal"
Yet the words never set in stone.

From the very roots of origins
When white ceased to exist
It never dawned upon them
That being black would be a sin
Years of torture years of climbing back
All for the sake of getting to an equal track
When will cease to be white vs black?

The kidnapping from countries
Slaves to be sold
Bullies that have been told
"To change my skin is not an ability I hold"
We have seen protesting for decades
Knees to the neck
For the mistake, they could check
We heard the cry and threw up our fist
yet colorism still exists.

All this pain
Still yet to claim the equality they've been chasing
There should be no discrimination
For simply being black, white, or colored.

Black vs White
A feud they fight
For no reason at all
Even rain can fall on the lightest days
And flowers can bloom on the darkest
All shades and colors are beautiful
A trait we shall embrace
We should never face judgment for the color on our
skin.

51. I HAD CHASED IT FOR YEARS

Eyes forward
Toward the future
Always toward the future.

Till my legs were shattered
All the stairs I climbed
Stones and pebbles, I had stepped on.

Crumbled beneath my feet
A dream without discipline
A fight never fought.

Never aware of its current standing
Never living the moment
Till the lines ended.

Eyes forward
Toward the future
I had chased.

52. HYPOCRITES

So quick
To bring the stick
You hypocrite.

Humans are filthy
Filthy indeed
Favor their selves over any breed
To watch the other cry and crumble
FILTHY, FILTHY, FILTHY.

We were a pair
A group of two
I had trust
Trust in you
Swore to be fair
Swear no more
Because you broke the promise
The promise you swore
GUILTY, GUILTY, GUILTY.

You tricked me
You tricky witch
50/50
Why'd you switch
I despise you
You boil my blood
But you watch and smirk

Cause it's me bleeding
FILTHY, FILTHY, FILTHY.

I take the blame
Waiting for you
Your voice
Yeah, a second soon
But silence remains
I take all the pain
GUILTY, GUILTY, GUILTY.

Grit my teeth
Clench my jaw
You lost my trust
All above all
You watch me sink
Guilty freak
FILTHY, FILTHY, FILTHY.
Humans are filthy
Filthy indeed
Favor their selves over any breed
To watch the other cry and crumble
GUILTY, GUILTY, GUILTY.

So quick
To bring the stick
You hypocrite.

Filthy, guilty beings
Yes indeed.

53. BALANCE

I, the weight of the world
Which remains nothing
The choice of good and bad
I give the outcome.

I, between heavens and hells
I, the one that holds the next life
I, the sight of future and past
The present
The key of the mind and body.

I, the one that lives upon the lord's palms
To join me as fellow acquaintance
Splendid destiny indeed
For those that turn a shoulder
Believe to face me.

I, between chaos and harmony
Death and life
Destruction and construction.

I, as still as water
As feisty as fire
For balance is me.

Available on www.amazon.com and many other outlets.
Montreal - April 2021.

9 782924 928158